DIGITAL CITIZENS

MY
DIGITAL FUTURE

By Ben Hubbard
Illustrated by Diego Vaisberg

W
FRANKLIN WATTS
LONDON • SYDNEY

Franklin Watts
First published in Great Britain in 2018 by
The Watts Publishing Group
Copyright © The Watts Publishing
Group 2018

Credits
Series Editor: Julia Bird
Illustrator: Diego Vaisberg
Packaged by: Collaborate

ISBN 978 1 4451 5863 1

Franklin Watts
An imprint of
Hachette Children's Group
Part of The Watts Publishing Group
Carmelite House
50 Victoria Embankment
London EC4Y 0DZ

An Hachette UK Company
www.hachette.co.uk
www.franklinwatts.co.uk

Printed in China

MIX
Paper from
responsible sources
FSC® C104740
FSC
www.fsc.org

CONTENTS

What is digital citizenship?   4

Future technology today   6

Dating digital devices   8

The latest thing   10

Digital maintenance   12

Explaining the world   14

Online shopping   16

Technology in business   18

Technology in schools   20

Educating the world   22

Technology tomorrow   24

The future is unwritten   26

Digital quiz   28

Glossary and helpful websites   30

Index   32

WHAT IS DIGITAL CITIZENSHIP?

When we log onto the internet we become part of a giant, online world.

In this world we can use our smartphones, tablets and computers to explore, create and communicate with billions of different people. Together, these people make up a global digital community. That is why they are known as digital citizens. When you use the internet you are a digital citizen too. So what does this mean?

CITIZEN VS DIGITAL CITIZEN

A good citizen is someone who behaves well, looks after themselves and others, and tries to make their community a better place. A good digital citizen acts exactly the same way. However, the online world is bigger than just a local neighbourhood, city or country. It spans the whole world and crosses every kind of border. It is therefore up to all digital citizens everywhere to make this digital community a safe, fun and exciting place for everyone.

MY DIGITAL FUTURE

Digital technology is how we manage our lives in the modern world. Many people stay logged-in to the internet, their networks and the wider online community using mobile and wearable devices. Keeping up-to-date with trends in digital technology is an important part of being a digital citizen. The future, after all, will be digital. But what developments might this bring? This book explores the world of digital technology today and how it might look tomorrow.

DID YOU INVENT THAT? WHAT IS IT?

A TRANSPORTER THAT TAKES ME TO ANY PLACE I SEE ONLINE. I'M OFF TO VISIT THE DINOSAURS.

WON'T THAT BE DANGEROUS?

THAT'S WHY I'VE ALSO INVENTED THIS FLYING INVISIBILITY BUBBLE. IT'S BITE-PROOF!

FUTURE TECHNOLOGY TODAY

In the modern world we are surrounded by digital technology.

There are smartphones, tablets and wearable devices wherever we go. Our homes contain computers, gaming consoles and smart appliances. The internet is what connects all of these devices and the people who use them. In the future, however, it will make us more connected than ever before.

SMART FAMILIES

Today, families often communicate by sending instant messages and emails or checking social media posts. Sometimes they do this even while they are in the same home! Some homes, however, have taken their digital technology to the next level with 'smart' appliances that are connected to the internet. This means lights, ovens and security systems can control themselves or be managed remotely from a smartphone. Sometimes, these appliances are linked to a central 'hub' robot that can walk around, talk and recognise household members.

THE INTERNET OF THINGS

Smart appliances in the home are part of the Internet of Things (IoT). This refers to connected devices that talk to each other and us over the internet. An example is a smart fridge that messages us when it is running out of milk. However, in the future the IoT is predicted to operate on a much bigger scale than just home appliances. This could mean fitness collars that would tell us when to exercise our dogs, smartbins that message the council when they are full and traffic lights that interact with our self-driving cars to ensure no-one gets caught in traffic.

DATING DIGITAL DEVICES

The rate of technology is moving so fast that new digital devices seem to go out of date almost as soon as they are unveiled.

However, staying informed about new technologies is an important part of being a digital citizen. So what digital trends are predicted for the near future?

ROBOTS ABOUT

Robots have been all around us now for many years. There are robots working in factories, hospitals and homes at this very moment. There have been robot pets for decades and it may not be long before we see robot assistants in shops and restaurants.

EXCUSE ME MISS, WHAT IS A 'SMARTPHONE'?

MORE REALITY

Virtual Reality (VR) headsets were often first used in gaming. They allowed users to see and interact in virtual 3D worlds like they were actually there. However, VR headsets can now also be used to: browse, buy and use apps; design aircraft and cars; and explore simulated environments on Earth. It is predicted VR will soon be used to interact with live environments and other people — all from the comfort of your home. This could mean having front row seats at a sports match, attending school lessons or visiting your doctor, all by simply putting on a VR headset.

WEAR IT WELL

Wearable digital technology allows us to access the internet from devices such as smart watches or glasses, avoiding the need for a digital device that we carry around. Controlling our devices by voice is also a new way of cutting back on screen use. It is predicted that smart glasses or headsets controlled by our voices could soon beam images directly into our eyes. This could one day make smartphones a gadget of the past.

DRONE DELIVERIES

In 2016, the first pizzas were delivered by drone. Now, new drones are being developed that deliver people! These drones are being designed to pick people up and fly them to work or school without them having to steer. Maybe the future for young digital citizens will include attending school lessons via a VR headset while being taken from place to place by personal drone!

THE LATEST THING

As consumers of new technology, digital citizens are often urged to 'buy, buy, buy'.

Technology companies constantly compete to release the latest gadget and their adverts insist we cannot do without it. An important part of being a digital citizen is understanding how to use today's technology. But how can we stay digitally literate without being pressured to purchase the 'latest thing'?

DON'T BELIEVE THE HYPE

Clever digital citizens know how to keep up-to-date with new technology without having to actually buy it. This is easily achieved by doing some research online. Reading online technology magazines and watching reviews of new gadgets is a great first step. This can keep you in the loop without having to spend money.

GREATEST, NOT LATEST

It's easy to see a new gadget advertised and fool ourselves into believing we can't live without it. However, with time this passes. After all, does your current gadget still work? Then why replace it? It's also important to realise the latest thing is not always the greatest thing. It's best to ignore our impulses to buy things and instead carefully evaluate what we need and what we don't. This is how clever digital citizens avoid being sucked into a never-ending buying loop.

IT CAN'T EVEN RECEIVE EMAILS!

I LOVE IT!

THAT'S SO RETRO.

DIGITAL MAINTENANCE

Have you ever lost or broken your smartphone or tablet? It can be a bitter blow.

Sometimes, it's only when these devices are gone that we realise how much we use them. That's why smart digital citizens take care of their digital devices and keep them in good working order. These tips can show you how.

WHAT'S THAT YOU'VE GOT?

THIS IS A STEEL-REINFORCED, LEAD-LINED PROTECTION BOX FOR MY MOBILE. IT SHOULD NOW BE ABLE TO SURVIVE A NUCLEAR BLAST.

CASE PROTECTED

Buying a case for your digital device and a screen protector is a good, simple form of protection. These will keep your devices from becoming scratched and may save them from being broken if they are dropped.

SAFE STORAGE

Have a safe spot where you keep your digital device when it is not in use, such as a bookshelf. Keep your charger there too. This will keep your device from being sat or trodden on and also can help prevent you misplacing it.

PRESERVE YOUR BATTERY

Mobile batteries can last years if properly looked after. The best way of doing this is to charge them regularly. Experts say keeping your mobile battery at between 40 per cent and 80 per cent will greatly increase its life. A simpler tip is to try not to let your phone's battery drop below a 40 per cent charge.

DRY, NOT WET

It may seem obvious, but don't get your device wet by using it in the rain. Also be extra careful around open water, such as rivers, the sea and toilets!

IN SIGHT, OUT OF MIND

Never let your device out of sight when in public. Also make sure you have set a passcode on your device in case it ever gets stolen. This will prevent a thief accessing your information. You can even download anti-theft software to shut down and locate your phone if it is stolen. Ask your trusted adult for help with this.

UPDATE SOFTWARE

Carrying out software updates on your digital device can stop it being infected by viruses or malware. This is because software updates are often released soon after new harmful bugs and viruses have been detected. Software updates almost always improve your phone's performance too.

EXPLAINING THE WORLD

Blogs, instructional videos and video blogs (vlogs) are an excellent way to learn from the experts online.

These can give us information about how things work, or hands-on advice on building things. They can also provide us with walkthroughs of online games and reviews of the latest technology. They can help us become both capable digital citizens and also informed consumers.

HOW TO DO IT...

Have you ever dreamed about making a smartphone projector? Or perhaps a simple robot? It's easy to learn how with instructional videos. Simply type what you'd like to make into a video-sharing website or a general search engine.

USEFUL REVIEWS

Part of being a smart digital citizen is staying informed about the latest digital technology and what it promises to do. It's easy to find reviews on a new product by entering its name and 'review' into a search engine. Reviews often show that the latest thing isn't what it's cracked up to be, which can save you a lot of money and heartache.

GAME WALKTHROUGHS

All gamers know the frustration of being defeated at a difficult point in a game — over and over and over again. Walkthroughs of video games can help immensely with these tricky bits. They can also offer cheats if you've really had enough of doing it the honest way. Simply drop your game's name and 'walkthrough' or 'cheat' into a search engine.

"It's too expensive, it doesn't have a headphone jack, and it is no better than the previous model. Avoid!"

ONLINE SHOPPING

Shopping online is so popular that many people use it for almost all of their purchases.

It is possible to buy virtually anything online, but shopping this way can present some risks. Fake websites are a common danger. However, clever digital citizens know how to spot a fake website so they won't get scammed.

THIS ONE'S SUPER CHEAP.

PERHAPS IT'S TOO GOOD TO BE TRUE. DID YOU LOOK AT THE 'SPOT THE FAKE WEBSITE' CHECKLIST?

SPOT THE FAKE WEBSITE

You've found a website that offers the same products as elsewhere, but for much lower prices. Sound too good to be true? It probably is. Investigate the website by following this checklist:

1 Does it have broken English, spelling mistakes, or odd-sounding text?

2 Has the website's domain name been recently registered? Have a look by using a 'domain-name lookup'. Your trusted adult can help with this.

SPOT THE FAKE REVIEW

Sometimes fake websites post fake reviews to convince people that they are genuine. If there are a number of reviews that have been recently posted, this can be a sign that the reviews are fake. If the reviews are short, do not give much information and are all worded in the same way, this can be another tell-tale sign. If you find any such reviews about a website it is probably best to steer clear of it altogether.

SO CHEEP

!

BY NOW!

SUMER SALE!

MUM, YOU WERE RIGHT. THIS WEBSITE LOOKS LIKE A FAKE.

3 Does the website have any contact details, such as a phone number, street address or email address?

4 Is there a 'returns' page with a clear returns policy?

5 Has anyone had trouble with the website before? Check this out by dropping the website's name and the word 'review' or 'genuine?' into a search engine. If the answers to any of these questions are 'yes', avoid it!

TECHNOLOGY IN BUSINESS

Digital technology has been of great benefit to businesses.

Twenty years ago, an office worker making a video conference call via their smartphone would have been unthinkable. Today it is commonplace. Now, young digital entrepreneurs are making a name for themselves by creating new social media platforms, apps and games. Others are using digital technology to address environmental issues affecting our planet.

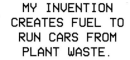

> MY INVENTION CREATES FUEL TO RUN CARS FROM PLANT WASTE.

FOR THE GREATER GOOD

Although many digital entrepreneurs have made millions, not all are motivated by money. Many want to use digital technology to help people and save the planet. Some do this by using the internet to raise awareness for the work they do. Others invent new technologies to help people in need. Some examples of these follow.

GREEN APPS

There are green apps available that help people become more environmentally minded. These include apps that scan barcodes to tell you where a product comes from and if its manufacture harms the environment. Another records your carbon footprint and suggests ways of cutting it down.

ONLINE ENTREPRENEURS

Entrepreneurs have looked for ways of making money from the internet since it was launched. Social media platforms have made many people extremely rich, as have apps and online games. Some of those behind new social media platforms, apps and games are only in their teens.

BIO-FUEL COULD POWER MANY OF THE WORLD'S VEHICLES INSTEAD OF POLLUTING PETROL.

SMART SAVINGS

Smart homes run by a central computer or robot connected to the internet aim to eliminate energy waste in the home. They do this by switching off lights when nobody is in the room, using appliances at night when energy is cheaper and powering down any appliance that is not in active use.

SPREAD THE WORD

Video websites that feature inspiring speakers are easy to find on the internet. Some of these sites have an emphasis on tackling environmental issues and keeping the world green. Such video sites raise awareness, help people collaborate and make us think about the issues facing the world.

TECHNOLOGY IN SCHOOLS

Schools around the world use digital technology differently.

Some schools have no digital technology at all. Others have strict rules about how it can be used. The best schools are those which use digital technology to develop collaborative projects with pupils. These projects can help spread the word about being a good digital citizen.

SOCIALLY RESPONSIBLE

Social media sites sometimes receive negative press because they can be used by pupils to bully others. But they can also be used to spread anti-bullying messages. The pupils of one US school used social media to discuss why bullying is wrong and also define what it means to be a good digital citizen. The group described a good digital citizen as: 'An individual who is aware, empathetic and socially responsible, both face-to-face and online.' The pupils then shared their findings via video conferencing with different schools and a panel of adult education experts.

MEET YOUR PUPILS

A group of digital educators in the US have created a social media website that shares the views of both teachers and pupils. Articles and vlogs about being digital citizens can then be viewed by others. This helps pupils feel their opinions are valued too.

EDUCATING THE WORLD

Clever digital citizens want to live in a world of online users who can use technology well.

This means helping other people to use their digital devices. Many older people were not surrounded by online technology when they were growing up. This means they can sometimes need younger people to help them.

LET ME SHOW YOU HOW TO USE IT, DAD.

BE A GOOD DIGITAL TEACHER

The followings tips can help you become a good digital teacher, even with adults that can't use their digital devices properly!

DON'T ASSUME

Some people have never heard of social media or mobile apps! If you're showing someone how to do something online, don't assume they will understand what any of the names mean.

GETTING THE BASICS

If you're showing someone how to do something online, just teach them the basics first. Otherwise it's easy for them to get overwhelmed. Once they've got it, you can show them more.

PRAISE IS GOOD

Even adults need to be told that they are doing a good job sometimes! Saying things like 'That's good' and 'You've got it' can make a big difference.

BE PATIENT

Everyone learns in different ways, so it's important not to get irritated if someone doesn't understand something straight away.

KEEP LEARNING

There's always more to learn about online technology and smart digital citizens make sure they are up-to-date with what's new. Never feel afraid to ask someone about new technology.

TECHNOLOGY TOMORROW

Many people worry that technology is ruling our lives.

They say the digital devices that were created as tools now control us. How much we should allow new technology into our lives is a question all digital citizens should consider. This will help form our ideas about future technology.

BECOMING CYBORGS

After we tire of smartphones and wearable technology, experts predict that people will turn to digital implants. This could include having a surgically-added device that connects your brain directly to the internet. Another eye implant would enable you to bring up a screen in front of you whenever you like. For many this is too much like creating cyborgs — humans that are mixed with machines. What do you think?

CAN YOU SWITCH OFF?

Digital citizens can sometimes struggle to turn off their devices. However, the internet is going to become more of a feature in our lives, not less. How much you use this technology is for you to decide. Ask yourself: 'Is it harming my body, or my mind?' or 'Is it preventing me from doing other things I enjoy offline?' Most of all: 'Is it making me feel good?' If you are unsure why you are even spending time online, maybe it's time to turn off your digital devices and take a break.

THANKS. BUT HOW DID YOU SEND THEM?

I CONNECTED WITH MY WI-FI IMPLANT, LOOKED UP YOUR NUMBER ON MY EYEBALL SCREEN AND WROTE A MESSAGE USING MY BRAIN WAVES. IT'S ALL THOUGHT-CONTROLLED IN THE FUTURE!

THE FUTURE IS UNWRITTEN

Nobody knows for sure what will come next in our digital world.

That is why it is important for digital citizens to discuss what being a good digital citizen means. Most agree that good digital citizens have certain qualities. These include trustworthiness, caring and empathy. But what are the other qualities? What do you think? After all, the digital future is a blank page ready to be written by citizens like you.

DIGITAL CITIZENS TO DIGITAL CREATORS

Perhaps it seems strange to list the qualities that digital citizens should have, but that's because young digital citizens of today like you will be the digital creators of tomorrow. This means you'll be deciding what kind of place the online world will be and how digital citizens should behave within it. With your help, the online world will be a safe, fun and exciting place for all!

Good digital citizens should:

1 Respect themselves and other people online.

2 Protect themselves and the personal information of people around them.

3 Believe in free speech, as long as it doesn't hurt others.

WHAT ELSE SHOULD DIGITAL CITIZENS BE LIKE? I'M DRAWING A BLANK!

IF YOU CAN'T THINK OF ANY NEW QUALITIES HAVE A LOOK THROUGH YOUR BOOK!

Can you think of any other qualities to add to this list?

4 Respect the law and the digital rules of their parents and school

5 Show kindness, caring and compassion to other digital citizens.

6 Believe everyone should have access to the internet.

7 Look after their physical and mental wellbeing while they are online.

DIGITAL QUIZ

Now you've reached the end of this book how do you feel about your digital future?

How much have you learned? And how much can you remember? Take this quiz and tally up your score at the end to find out.

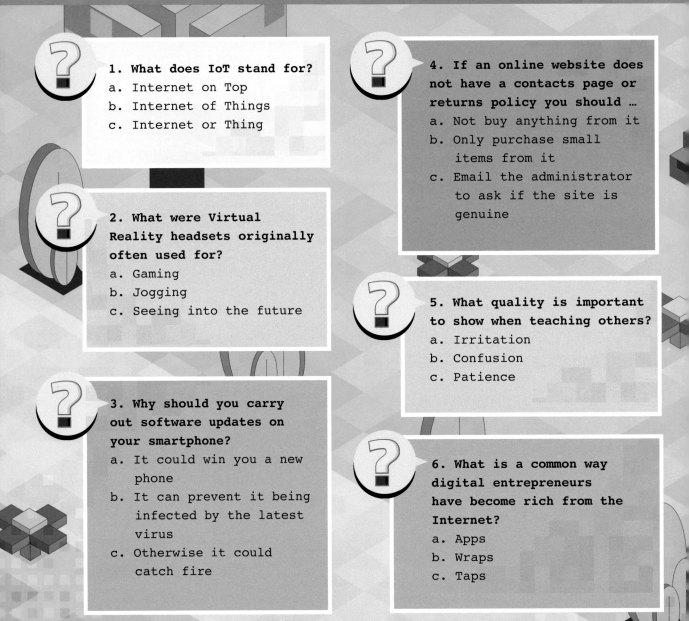

1. What does IoT stand for?
a. Internet on Top
b. Internet of Things
c. Internet or Thing

2. What were Virtual Reality headsets originally often used for?
a. Gaming
b. Jogging
c. Seeing into the future

3. Why should you carry out software updates on your smartphone?
a. It could win you a new phone
b. It can prevent it being infected by the latest virus
c. Otherwise it could catch fire

4. If an online website does not have a contacts page or returns policy you should …
a. Not buy anything from it
b. Only purchase small items from it
c. Email the administrator to ask if the site is genuine

5. What quality is important to show when teaching others?
a. Irritation
b. Confusion
c. Patience

6. What is a common way digital entrepreneurs have become rich from the Internet?
a. Apps
b. Wraps
c. Taps

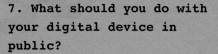

7. What should you do with your digital device in public?

a. Show it off
b. Ask strangers to hold it
c. Never let it out of your sight

8. What might replace smartphones in the future?

a. Digital implants
b. Tin cans
c. Robots that we can talk into

HOW DID YOU DO? ADD UP YOUR SCORE TO SEE.

1-4: You are on your way but retake the quiz to get a score over 4.

5-7: You've passed the quiz well. Now see if you can pass the quiz in the book *My Community and Media.*

8: Wow! 8 out of 8. You are a natural born digital citizen!

ANSWERS

1: b; 2: a; 3: b; 4: a; 5: a; 6: c; 7: a; 8: a

GLOSSARY

Apps
Short for 'applications', apps are computer programmes for mobile digital devices, such as smart phones or tablets.

Carbon footprint
The amount of harmful carbon dioxide that is released into the atmosphere as a result of one person's activities.

Cyberbullying
Bullying that takes place online or using internet-based apps.

Digital
Technology that involves computers.

Download
To take information or files from the internet and store them on your computer.

Internet
The vast electronic network that allows billions of computers from around the world to connect to each other.

Malware
A dangerous computer programme that is created to damage or disable other digital devices.

Online
Being connected to the internet via a computer or digital device.

Passcode
A password made up of numbers or letters that prevents access to your digital device.

Search engine
A computer programme that carries out a search of available information on the internet based on the words you type in.

Smartphone
A mobile phone that is capable of connecting to the internet.

Social media
Websites that allow users to share content and information online.

Trusted adult
An adult you know well and trust who can help you with all issues relating to the internet.

Virtual reality (VR)
Computer generated environment that people can interact with.

Website
A collection of web pages that is stored on a computer and made available to people over the internet.

HELPFUL WEBSITES

Digital Citizenship
The following websites have helpful information about digital citizenship for young people:

http://www.digizen.org/kids/

http://www.digitalcitizenship.nsw.edu.au/Prim_Splash/

http://www.cyberwise.org/digital-citizenship-games

http://www.digitalcitizenship.net/Nine_Elements.html

Staying Safe
These websites are dedicated to keeping kids safe online, with lots of good advice:

http://www.childnet.com/young-people/primary

http://www.kidsmart.org.uk

http://www.safetynetkids.org.uk/personal-safety/staying-safe-online/

http://www.bbc.co.uk/newsround/13910067

Bullying
These websites have excellent advice for kids who are experiencing bullying online. There also some helplines, which children can call anonymously to receive expert advice:

https://www.childline.org.uk/info-advice/bullying-abuse-safety/types-bullying/online-bullying/

Childline helpline for kids: 0800 1111

http://www.bullying.co.uk

BullyingUK helpline for kids: 0808 800 2222

https://www.stopbullying.gov/kids/facts/

https://www.commonsensemedia.org/videos/cyberbullying-prevention-guide-for-kids

INDEX

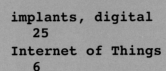

advertising,
    resisting 10—11
appliances, smart 6
apps, green 18

batteries,
    preserving 12
bullying 21

consumerism 10—11
cyborgs 25

devices, protecting
    12—13
drones 9

entrepreneurs,
    digital 18—19
environment 18—19

gaming 8, 14—15
glasses, smart 9

headsets, Virtual
    Reality 8—9
homes, smart 6, 19

implants, digital
    25
Internet of Things
    6

passcodes 13

reviews, using 11,
    14, 17
robots 6, 8, 14, 19

schools 20—21
switching off 25

teaching 22—23

updates, software
    13

videos,
    instructional
    14—15
vlogs 14, 21

walkthroughs 14—15
watches, smart 9
websites, fake
    16—17

Health & Wellness
- What is digital citizenship?
- Your digital health and wellness
- Prepare to prevent pain
- Stretch, don't strain
- Digital training
- App attack
- Online time limits
- Online addiction
- Social media and self-image
- Avoiding adverts
- Being boys and girls
- Digital detox
- Digital quiz

Rights & Rules
- What is digital citizenship?
- Know your rights
- Rule of the tools
- Information invasion
- Free speech
- Protecting others, protecting yourself
- Privacy particulars
- Digital law
- Original online work
- Illegal downloads
- Access for all
- Help everyone participate
- Digital quiz

My Digital World
- What is digital citizenship?
- Connect, collect and communicate
- A world of websites
- Cyber searching
- Digital friendships
- To share or not to share?
- Messaging aware
- Phone etiquette
- Cyberbullying
- Bystanding
- Send a cyber smile
- A world outside
- Digital quiz

My Digital Future
- What is digital citizenship?
- Future technology today
- Dating digital devices
- The latest thing
- Digital maintenance
- Explaining the world
- Online shopping
- Technology in business
- Technology in schools
- Educating the world
- Technology tomorrow
- The future is unwritten
- Digital quiz

My Digital Community and Media
- What is digital citizenship?
- Social society
- My networks
- Gaming groups
- Hobbies and interests
- Netiquette
- Kindness, not cruelty
- Online news
- Spot the fake
- I am a brand
- Uniting online
- Shrinking the world
- Digital quiz

My Digital Safety and Security
- What is digital citizenship?
- Prepare to protect
- Trusted help
- Protecting personal details
- Passwords and Passcodes
- Cyberbullies and trolls
- Private social media
- Cyber strangers
- I'm in trouble
- Cyber criminals
- Pop-ups and pitfalls
- Viruses and malware
- Digital quiz